DRAWING MAMMALS

Fox
Chapel Publishing Co. Inc.

1970 Broad Street • East Petersburg, PA 17520 • www.carvingworld.com

DRAWING MAMMALS

by Doug Lindstrand

Dedicated, with love, to my sisters:
JoAnn, Joyce, and Karen.

Library of Congress Catalog Card Number 99–94353
ISBN 1–56523–206–2

10 9 8 7 6 5 4 3 2 1

To order your copy of this book,
please send check or money order
for the cover price plus $3.00 shipping to:
Fox Chapel Publishing Company Inc.
Book Orders
1970 Broad Street
East Petersburg, PA 17520

Or visit our website at
www.carvingworld.com

Printed in China

Other Doug Lindstrand Books:
Alaska Sketchbook, 200 pages, ISBN 1-56523-142-2
Drawing America's Wildlife, 216 pages, ISBN 0-9608290-6-7
Drawing Big Game, ISBN 1-56523-140-6

INDEX

POLAR BEAR / CUBS

Adult male
Yukon Territory
October

GRAY WOLF / MALE

6

FORWARD

The goal of this book is to portray twenty "favorite" North American mammals in various poses, ages, and seasons. The artist drew the animals dimensions as accurately as possible, and by adding photographs and biological text, hopes his endeavor will be helpful to other artists, carvers, etc.

So then, from the noble Gray wolf of the Yukon Territory to the tiny Key deer of Florida, the "reference guide" titled "DRAWING MAMMALS" by Doug Lindstrand.

FLORIDA "KEY" DEER / BUCK (NOVEMBER)

This is my field-pack contents: sketchbook, pencils (my "favorite" is HB charcoal), French stumps, sharpening tools, kneaded erasers, spray fixative, tape, rulers, pastels, and binoculars.

The artist's "roving studio". A motorhome/camper makes a great "base camp". From these comfortable headquarters you can make daily (or longer) treks afield. Then, upon return, have a place to resupply, draw, sleep and shower. Naturally, when your treks keep you away overnight, it is smart to either park in a secure area or have someone keep-an-eye on it for you.

INTRODUCTION

Drawing, to me, is one of the basic tools of an artist's foundation. From a limited mastering of this medium, one can better pursue all other artistic endeavors from painting to sculpting. One only has to look back in history to men such as Michelangelo, da Vinci, and Picasso to fully appreciate how their drawing talents enabled them to ultimately produce artwork that, after all these years, still touches and inspires us all. The magnificent ceilings of the Sistine chapel, the mysterious *Mona Lisa,* and the controversial *Guernica* all probably started with a few scribbles on a scrap of paper. The pencil, then, is to an artist what a hammer is to a carpenter: a useful and necessary tool. How far you wish to pursue "building your house" of drawing skills will be a personal choice, but to some of us, it has become a preferred medium with which to portray our subjects. You can, believe it or not, actually make a living chasing wild animals around the woods with pencil and paper in hand.

This *Drawing Mammals* book is a portfolio of charcoal drawings, notes, and photographs that were compiled via my travels around North America. It was an exciting project, a true adventure. Canada, Mexico, and the United States are truly wondrous lands filled with magnificent wildlife. I hope you, too, will someday take the time and effort to explore and appreciate North America for yourselves. In fact, I hereby ASSIGN IT as homework to all artists. After all, obtaining original reference material is a must for any person who hopes to sell his artwork or make art a career choice. There is no substitute for being in the field with your quarry. Then, once you have acquired this knowledge and material via your observations, photographs, notes, and field sketches, you can confidently and accurately portray the animal back at your studio. I sincerely hope you find fun and satisfaction with your drawing and, if you so desire, a market for your creations. We are living in an era where wildlife and wilderness are appreciated, and more and more people are choosing scenes of wildlife and wilderness to decorate their homes and businesses. It is a way, perhaps, of bringing the tranquil sense of nature into our hearts and minds. Historically, there has never been a time when nature artists and photographers were more in demand.

Doug Lindstrand

AN INTERVIEW WITH THE ARTIST

For the past 30 years, Alaskan-at-heart Doug Lindstrand has been capturing America's wildlife on film and canvas. Here, in a special interview with the author, Doug tells of his first "sighting" of his future home, his inspirations, his dreams, and the message he hopes to convey through his art. He also shares tried-and-true tips for aspiring wildlife photographers.

<u>Why Alaska?</u> In 1967 I made a stop-over in Alaska en route to Vietnam. As my plane circled and made its approach to landing in Anchorage, I saw along the shores of a frozen lake a lone little cabin with a column of smoke rising from its chimney. This "scene" stayed in my memory throughout my military tour in Southeast Asia, and it served as a goal for when I again returned stateside. In 1970, after an art and biology degree from college and a short stint as a commercial artist, I decided to travel to either Australia or Alaska to freelance. Because Alaska seemed somewhat closer to my Minnesota home (and Mom's famous blueberry pie), I chose Alaska. I left my Corvette convertible with my sister to sell, bought a 4WD Bronco, and headed for the Last Frontier. I became that person who built fires in remote cabins. For the first five winters I lived alone in wilderness cabins to work on my art and to observe wildlife. Alaska is truly a paradise for a nature/wildlife artist as it is impossible to run out of inspiration and subjects.

<u>Does one need to have an art degree to draw wildlife?</u> As for actual drawing instruction, I prefer to leave that to each artist to discover for himself, and to the dozens of art books that might be useful to beginners wishing to learn more about composition and perspective. Because I have always had an interest in wildlife, I wanted to have a profession and education that would keep me in contact with animals—either through my art or else as a biologist or researcher—hence my degree in art and biology.

<u>When is the best time to photograph animals?</u> Because most animals are in their "prime" during either Spring or Autumn, those are my favorite times to take pictures of wildlife in their natural habitats. In the Spring, many birds are in their colorful mating plumage, and it is also the time for the birth of most young. Autumn is when antlered big game animals sport their magnificent "racks" and have grown their thicker cold-weather coats. A bull elk, for example, looks so much more regal and impres-

FIELD-SKETCH TO FINAL DRAWING

✳✳The following is an example of how I'll turn a field-sketch or doodle into a final drawing. I use field-sketching to capture an idea, pose, or "essence" of something in nature. I seldom do much detail in the field, preferring my studio for that. Also, <u>to better illustrate these "steps"</u>, I transferred the transparent paper "refinements" to regular paper in order to photograph it for this book.

<u>STEP 1</u>
Field-sketch.

← Selected image.

<u>STEP 2</u>
   <u>Lay transparent paper over your field-sketch and trace the main lines.</u> Then lay another sheet of transparent paper over the first and continue this "refining" until the dimensions are suitable.

<u>STEP 3</u>
   <u>Flip over your "final" refinement and pencil along the main lines.</u> Then flip it back over, position it on the drawing paper or illustration board, and then "rub" the lines in order to transfer the image.

11

STEP 4

You now have the outline of your animal transferred. You may have to slightly darken the transfer lines before beginning. After that, it's just a matter of filling in between-the-lines. Of course, surrounding you, will be your library of reference material (books, photos, field-sketches, etc.) to help if needed.

STEP 5

Being right handed, I begin my drawings at the left side in order to prevent smudging. I save putting in the darkest tones until the drawing is basically done. It's best to evaluate the entire drawing before choosing where to add the blackest blacks. Making these "steps" a part of your routine should help make your finished art more saleable; because you have done most of your "correcting" prior to reaching your illustration board or paper.

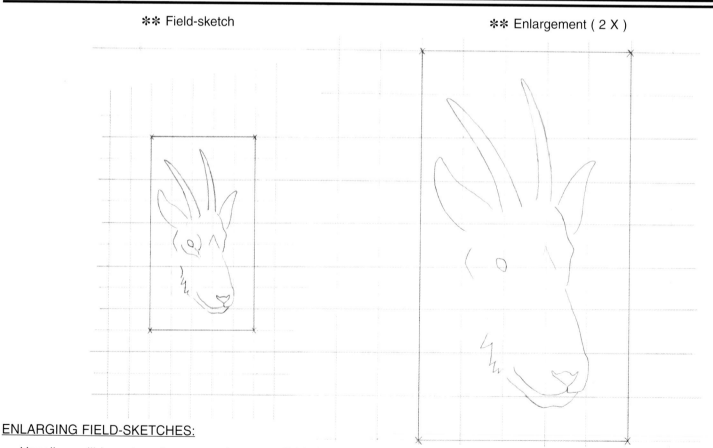

✳✳ Field-sketch   ✳✳ Enlargement (2 X)

ENLARGING FIELD-SKETCHES:

Usually you'll have to enlarge or reduce your field-sketches, and employing a grid of reference points should help guide you. (Naturally, the two grids must be proportional to one another.) This can be done at any stage prior to transferring the final refinement to your illustration board or paper. I, personally, normally make one refinement to help "shape the animal" prior to enlarging/reducing.

MOUNTAIN GOAT / NANNY

13

✳✳ I added this drawing to show that even though I follow a routine of "steps" to refine my field-sketches (prior to transferring the outline to my illustration board), sometimes they still "go bad". <u>This wolf pup's head is too big</u>! Even though I realized it sooner, I finished the drawing to illustrate the point. Once you realize that a drawing has "gone bad", don't waste time trying to "rescue" it. Scrap it, make your corrections, and begin anew.

✳✳ Outline of "original" drawing
from page 14.

✳✳ Outline of "corrected" drawing
(with slight changes).

✳✳ This is a beginning revision of the wolf pup. I reduced the head about 10%. Since I had a finished drawing to "play with", I made a copy on a copy machine, and then made other copies in various reductions. After cutting-and-pasting, I found a head size that fit the body. Nowadays all sorts of "tools" can be used to aid and simplify your artwork. This cutting-and-pasting (via a "5¢-a-copy" copy machine) was an effective and time-saving substitute to my normal "grid" enlarging / reducing method.

sive in his prime coat and long polished antlers than he does wearing his thin summer coat and sporting short velvet-covered antlers. Also, portraying animals at their best will help make the finished artwork more saleable.

<u>Is there a "typical" year for a wildlife photographer?</u> I don't think I could describe a typical year as each one since 1970 has been different. Although my distant past has been involved primarily with Alaska wildlife and people, lately I have also branched into "outside" subjects such as whitetails, mountain lions, quail, and other species that are not common to Alaska. My interest in wildlife is such that I am constantly searching for new creatures to watch, study, and portray. My best-selling prints and note cards, however, are still Alaska "sourdoughs," the old bearded gold prospectors, miners, and fur trappers of the last frontier. The romantic vision of an old sourdough mushing his team of dogs across a snowy wilderness or panning for gold in a mountain stream has proven to be a popular theme for much of my Alaska art. Perhaps the only thing "typical" that occurs is that I almost always spend most of the so-called warm months sketching and photographing and most of the cold months in my studio or traveling in a motor home drawing and painting from my acquired reference material.

<u>Where are the best places to find wildlife?</u> Wildlife, like gold, is "where you find it." North America is blessed with wildlife and with people who cherish and protect these magnificent creatures. One of our protected places are state and national parks, places where animals are not hunted and therefore are much more tolerant of humans. My guess is that over half of the photographs in Drawing Mammals were taken in national parks from Alaska to Mexico. Also, zoos are a great place to sit and work on your sketching skills.

<u>Do you have a favorite animal?</u> Although my "favorite" animal has varied from year to year, right now I'd have to say it is the Dall sheep. This pure-white, amber-horned creature is a true symbol of the North. During the past two years, I have spent more time in the mountains with these magnificent animals than with all the other North American animals combined. I can't help but marvel at how these sheep can exist in the rocky, seemingly barren environment they live in. Also, in areas where they are not hunted, they are very approachable. By "approachable," I mean that Dall sheep will become accustomed to hikers and photographers in areas where they have not been overly disturbed. They are normally a very non-aggressive animal, and if you leave them an uphill escape exit, they will graze and rest within a few feet of a sitting person. Newborn lambs are especially trustworthy. I have camped with bands of

sheep in the high-country and would often find them sleeping next to my tent "wind-break" when I arose in the morning.

<u>Tell us about your most dangerous moment in the field.</u> Since 1970, I have literally spent years in the field with wildlife. In my earlier years, I would do anything to get a photograph and didn't dwell too much on the danger involved. During the last decade or so, I have made a conscious decision to be safer and to also give the animals their space. Longer telephoto lenses aid this decision and still allow me to capture the detail and reference I desire.

In my past, I have been treed and chased by all manner of beasts: bull moose in rut, cow elk with calves, and a herd of bison have all sent me scrambling up nearby trees. These animals were all approached with the knowledge that these trees were nearby. Unknowingly approaching a grizzly bear on a kill, however, was surely my most dangerous moment and almost ended my career. When he came out from the brush at full charge, I turned and ran and was lucky enough to claw and pull myself up a cut-away bluff before he could reach me. The roots and snags gave me something to grab and climb on, but restricted him from doing the same. I could hear his clicking fangs below me for an eternity before he ambled away. Believe me, I was strongly tempted to leave my camera equipment behind, and retrieving it later that day was almost as scary as hanging on that bluff. Being a starving artist, however, made the retrieval of my equipment a necessity.

<u>What art medium do you prefer?</u> My preferred medium is the charcoal pencil. Although most of my sales are of paintings, I feel most comfortable doing my art in pencil. In one of my other books, Drawing America's Wildlife, I illustrate how I often turn detailed drawings into pastel and watercolor paintings. Although most artists thrive on experimenting with all manner of mediums, the majority will eventually restrict themselves to doing their art in a method they are most comfortable with and which allows them to make their livelihood.

<u>What do you draw on?</u> Although I grew up drawing on anything I could find, I now mainly do my finished drawings on illustration or watercolor board. I do a lot of sketchbook sketching to perfect the dimensions, composition, and such, and will then transfer these images to the boards. These boards also allow the drawing to be easily framed and possibly sold. I also use a "hard" charcoal pencil. Running this pencil across a surface that has a slightly rough texture also helps when drawing fur and feathers.

Can anyone expect to make a living from wildlife art/photography? My first answer to those that ask me this question is to say, "The first fifty years are the hardest!" Most people will do their art and photography merely as a hobby and only occasionally sell some of it. Making a living from your work is more difficult and does take a certain dedication to go along with your talent. I have sketched all my life and always knew that I would probably someday be employed as an artist. Since art (and sports) was something I enjoyed, it was easy to dedicate time and effort to it. After college, I worked in advertising for a few months until I had acquired a small grubstake and was able to finance my move to Alaska and become a freelance artist/photographer. I honestly don't know of anyone who enjoys his job more than I enjoy mine.

What kinds of equipment do you suggest for a wildlife photographer/artist in the field? Any sort of camera can aid you, but unless you have a very tame or cooperative animal, you will probably want a 35mm SLR (single lens reflex) camera fronted

Remember, computer programming or this. . .

Author photographing caribou bull. When photographing wildlife, you will sense when you are intruding into an animals "space". If they appear nervous or agitated, slowly back-off. In this photo, the lone bull came towards us because we had positioned ourselves overlooking a likely trail.

with a telephoto lens. My experience has taught me to prefer a major brand camera over the bargain brands. Also, I prefer zoom lenses, because they allow me to adjust the telephoto power to fit the situation. Because animals refuse to sit still, it is handy to be able to adjust the power instead of constantly changing lenses. Most times I seemingly have only a split-second to "shoot" an animal. Fumbling with changing lenses will lead to a lost opportunity. In my field pack, I carry two favorite lenses: a 70-210mm and a 75-300mm, each on a separate camera body. For photographing very distant or dangerous animals, such as bears and mountain lions, I carry a 600mm fixed lens.

I also carry a light and easy-to-operate tripod (to take advantage of those split-seconds) and a number of rolls of film. Film choice should be based on personal experimentation. In theory, the more powerful the lens, the faster the film. Higher speed films tend to not have the same quality as slower speed films, but they allow shots in poor light conditions, such as dawn and dusk, which are also the times when most animals are most active. I carry 100 ASA to 400 ASA film. Print or slide film is also a personal choice. Magazine editors usually prefer slides, but print film is more forgiving regarding exposure.

Is there a message or a feeling that you hope to convey to people who see your artwork? Nowadays I think of myself more as an illustrator than as a fine artist. My real goal is to portray birds and mammals as accurately as possible so that other artists can confidently rely on my books for reference material. My art schooling has mostly been in oils, but my moves to various remote "bush cabins" throughout Alaska has made this medium difficult to dry, transport, and so on. Charcoal pencils, watercolors, and pastels have proved to be a more mobile and less difficult way of illustrating books. Upon retirement, however, I do plan to rekindle my love of "canvas and oils."

What are you working on now? I am currently gathering information for a series of reference books for artists. These "artist guide books" will give artists an in-depth look at a grouping of North American animals: deer, for example, or bear. It is my hope that an artist who is working on a painting or a drawing or a carving—any artistic endeavor in any medium that shows an animal—will be able to use these books to help him more accurately portray that animal. Anyone who's interested can check *www.foxchapelpublishing.com* or *www.douglindstrand.com* for updates.

You'll need a variety of equipment to photograph animals with. Pack your chosen gear into a comfortable pack. ALWAYS bring extra batteries and film. Nothing is more frustrating than being a million-miles-from-nowhere and running out of something.

20

TWENTY "FAVORITE" MAMMALS

BLACK BEAR

The Black bear (Ursus americanus) is the most abundant and widely dispersed of the three species of North American bears. States like Washington and Oregon have sizeable populations, while states like Nevada and Missouri have few. Their color ranges from the white Kermode bear of British Columbia to the more common cinnamon or black coated bears that roam elsewhere. The Yakutat area of Alaska has a small number of "blue" colored (or "glacier") Blacks. Also, many of the dark colored bears have a patch of white on their chests.

Black bears are the smallest of North America's bears. They are also the only bear here that can climb a tree as an adult. Males are larger than females and an adult "boar" is 39" - 40" at the shoulder and 50" - 75" from nose to tail. Weights vary widely, but 200 - 400#'s is the normal range. Black bears are distinguished from Brown bears by their straight facial profile, no shoulder "hump", and sharply curved claws.

Mating occurs from June through July and cubs are born in a den about seven months later. When the female (sow) emerges from her hibernation den in the Spring, she'll have one to four (5#) cubs at her side, and they'll nurse until winters hibernation comes again. In the wild a Black bear will live for about 15 years.

Black bears are creatures of opportunity regarding food. Although vegetation is their main food, they also are efficient predators and scavengers. Their scavenging "habits" are what usually brings them into conflict with humans. Where available, salmon and berries are an important source of nutrition.

Although no wild animal should be fed (except possibly in specific spots and for specific animals: example, the elk of Jackson Hole, Wyoming), bears especially should not be fed. Because of their unpredictable behavior, fed-bears often become dead-bears.

SOW (SEPTEMBER)

Claws are sharply curved and don't exceed 1½".
Black bears also lack the grizzlies shoulder "hump".

BLACK BEARS

23

BLACK BEAR/SOW (OCTOBER)

BLACK BEAR / BOAR (AUGUST)

25

BLACK BEAR / CUB (SEPTEMBER)

Adult track

Biologist holding Black bear cub
while doing research.
(early Spring)

The "Black" is the only North American
bear that can climb trees as an adult.
(Grizzly cubs can climb until about 1 year old.) 27

Height at shoulder - 3' - 3½ feet (mature adult)

Underside of front paw

Adult females average 150 - 300 pounds.
Weights vary widely amongst regions of America / Canada.

SOW TRACK

BLACK BEAR / SOWS

BROWN / GRIZZLY BEAR

The Brown/Grizzly bear (Ursus arctos) is a close relative of the Black bear, but is larger, has less noticeable ears, a more pronounced shoulder "hump", straighter claws, and a somewhat concave facial profile. "Brown" is used to refer to coastal area bears, whereas "grizzly" is used to refer to inland area bears. (Taxonomists do consider the Kodiak Island Brown bear as a distinct subspecie.) The Brown/Grizzly is a threatened/ endangered animal outside of Alaska and Canada. Montana, Wyoming and Idaho are about the only states south of the border that have meaningful populations. When human populations headed West, the "feared" beast was destroyed at every encounter until only a few now survive outside Alaska and Canada. Despite his phenomenal strength and courage, the "King" could not compete against the rifle.

Brown/Grizzlies colors range from light blond to dark brown. Males are larger than females and a mature Brown "boar" (after "fattening up" on salmon prior to denning) will often weigh over 1000 pounds. And although very large males can weigh 1500 pounds, the more average range is 500 - 800#'s. (Females (sows) weigh one-half to three-quarters as much.) Mature males are about 48" high at the shoulder and 60" - 80" from nose to tail. When standing on their hind feet, they measure about 8 feet tall.

Mating occurs from May through July and cubs (commonly two, and weighing about 1 pound) are born in the females winter den the following January/February. The cubs will often den with their mother for two winters before separating to establish their own territories. In the wild, a male will normally live about 20 years and the females about 25 years. Captive bears have lived over 45 years. The more northern bears often hibernate for over 6 months each year, while those living further south (such as Kodiak Island) may only hibernate for short periods of cold weather or food shortage. Pregnant females, of course, do den.

Brown/Grizzly bears are considered the most dangerous and unpredictable of all North American bears, so always use caution when hiking or photographing in grizzly country. Making noise and traveling in groups is the best protection against surprising one. Of course, when photographing, use long lenses. Especially keep a safe distance between you and sows with cubs; mating bears; and bears on a kill. Brown/Grizzlies are very aggressive and will attack if surprised or approached during any of these situations.

Brown/Grizzly bears are omnivorous and feed on anything from roots to insects to mammals. It is an efficient predator and often feeds on newborns, such as fawns and calves. Also, its phenomenal sense of smell enables it to detect carrion from miles away. During the summer's salmon-runs, the normally solitary creatures are often seen sharing streams with dozens of others, and take time from gorging to socialize and play-fight.

BROWN BEAR / BOAR (MAY)

30

Mature sow will weigh about ½ to ¾ as much as males.

FRONT PAW

Mature boar - about 4 feet at shoulder.

GRIZZLY / BROWN BEAR

31

TEETH SKETCH

"HUMP"

32 GRIZZLY / BROWN BEAR

BROWN BEAR / BOAR (MAY)

June

CUB
HIND FOOT

Born January - March in winter den.   Birth weight - less than 1 pound.

August

34   GRIZZLY / BROWN BEAR (CUBS)

May

Tracks

left hind

left front

October about 9 months old.

GRIZZLY / BROWN BEAR (CUBS)

35

36   GRIZZLY/BOAR (SEPTEMBER)

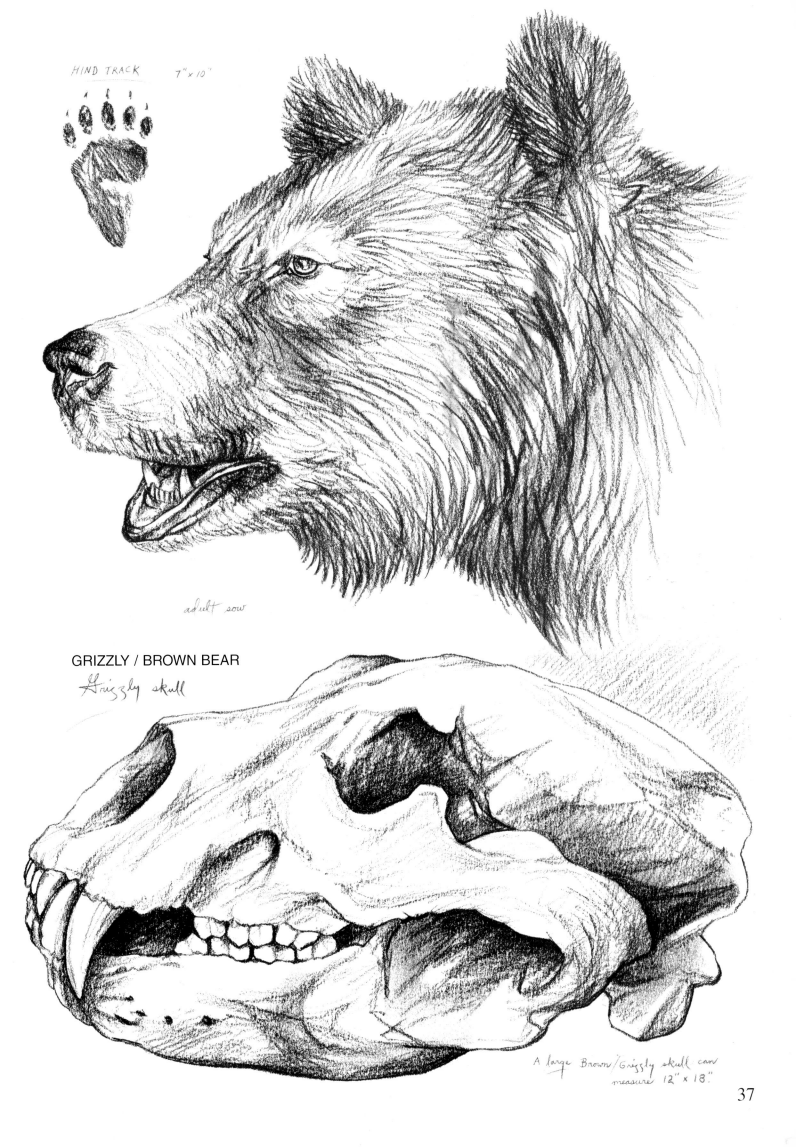

HIND TRACK   7" x 10"

adult sow

GRIZZLY / BROWN BEAR

Grizzly skull

A large Brown/Grizzly skull can measure 12" x 18".

37

Boar, Autumn coat

Front claws - 4" long

38   GRIZZLY / BROWN BEAR (BOAR)

GRIZZLY / BROWN BEAR

POLAR BEAR

The Polar bear (Ursus maritimus) occurs only in the northern hemisphere and is the regions top carnivore. Polar bears are closely related to Brown bears and large adults of both species are similar in weight; large males weighing 600 - 1500#'s and mature females weighing 450 - 700#'s. Males (boars) are about 48" high at the shoulder and average between 8 and 10 feet from nose to tail. This long necked, short eared Arctic denizen is distinguished by its white fur and black nose, eyes, and lips. It is a creature well suited for its environment.

Most Polar bears are solitary creatures, choosing to associate only during the mating season of April/May. The male then roams the sea ice from one receptive female to another. Fights between competing males are fierce and can end in death to one or both foes. Pregnant females (sows) seek out a winters den by November and usually gives birth in December. Litters of two are the most common and the mother and cubs emerge from their den in late Spring. By then the cubs weigh about 20 pounds and are able to keep up to the sows pace. It is a dangerous time for them, as roaming boars will attempt to kill newborn cubs. Older sows have learned to seek areas that hungry males do not frequent. Life expectancy is about 25 years in the wild.

Although most abundant near coastlines, the Polar bear roams widely and can occur throughout the Arctic basin. Their main food is ringed seals, but they are scavengers and their acute smelling prowess enables them to detect carrion from vast distances. Creatures such as whales or walrus often die as the result of an injury or wound and later wash up on shore or the ice pack. Polar bears are extremely patient and wily, and are able to stalk near enough to a careless, resting seal to slay it with a deadly swipe or bite. Or they may hover atop a "breathing hole" in the ice and ambush their prey.

CUBS (APRIL)

POLAR BEAR / SOWS

Adult Male
Hind track

13"

42   POLAR BEAR / CUB   (MAY)

CUBS/June

POLAR BEAR / CUBS   43

HIND TRACK

CUB / FRONT PAW TRACK

44   POLAR BEAR / CUBS

Cubs / Summer

POLAR BEAR / CUBS

Black - nose, eyes & lips.   Small ears, long neck.

POLAR BEARS

TOP: POLAR BEAR / CUB (MAY)   BOTTOM: POLAR BEAR / SOW (JUNE)   47

Mature females average 500 - 700 pounds.

Emerge from dens (with cubs) in March/April, when the cubs weigh 15-20 pounds.

10"

SOW TRACK

FRONT

48

POLAR BEAR / SOWS

POLAR BEAR / BOAR

COYOTE

The sly and adaptable coyote (Canis latrans) is a member of the dog family and inhabits most of America and the southern and western edges of Canada. Coyotes hunt alone, in pairs, and sometimes in packs. Pairs have been observed chasing prey (such as rabbits) in relays, whereas (since the prey normally runs in wide circles) a "fresh" coyote resumes the chase after the first one tires. If separated, the pair will communicate via a mournful howl that ends with a series of yips. This very vocal "song dog" also howls to pronounce territories.

The coyote has a slender, pointed nose, prominent ears, and a tail tipped in black. Grayish coat with areas of white (underside and upper lip), rust and tan. Average weights are 25 - 40#'s (about one-third the size of a northern wolf); shoulder height is about 24"; length (including tail) is 40" - 50".

Coyotes mate in February / April and the litter size is determined by the food supply available. If times are lean, few pups will be born. Pups normally leave their parents by winter, to hunt their main prey of rabbits (or hares) and rodents. Occasionally a pair of coyotes will hunt and kill larger mammals such as newborn pronghorn and deer.

Despite mans "war" on the coyote (hunting, poisoning, and trapping), the wily "song dog" continues to prosper and extend his range. Because of our continued march and development into the coyotes range, it is only natural that the coyote (and other wildlife) must adapt. That is why pets, livestock, and even young children are now being attacked on rare occasions.

ADULT FEMALE (FEBRUARY)

TRACKS
(roundish)

Pup

Autumn

WINTER
COAT

Pointed, slender snout.

Summer

COYOTES

WINTER COAT

IN SNOW
PAW PRINT

Pup

Long drawn-out howl

Study
Idaho

52   COYOTES

WINTER
WYOMING

Juvenile
Texas (February)

Pups
6-8 weeks

COYOTE / FEMALES & PUPS   53

54 COYOTE / MALE (JANUARY)

Erect ears

Tail usually ends
in a black
tip

average litter
5-7 pups

Pup.
First week out of den.

Adult male (average)
18-32 yds.
44-50" long
13-16" tail
22-26" tall

Track - Texas

CLAWS
SHOW →

(4" adult)

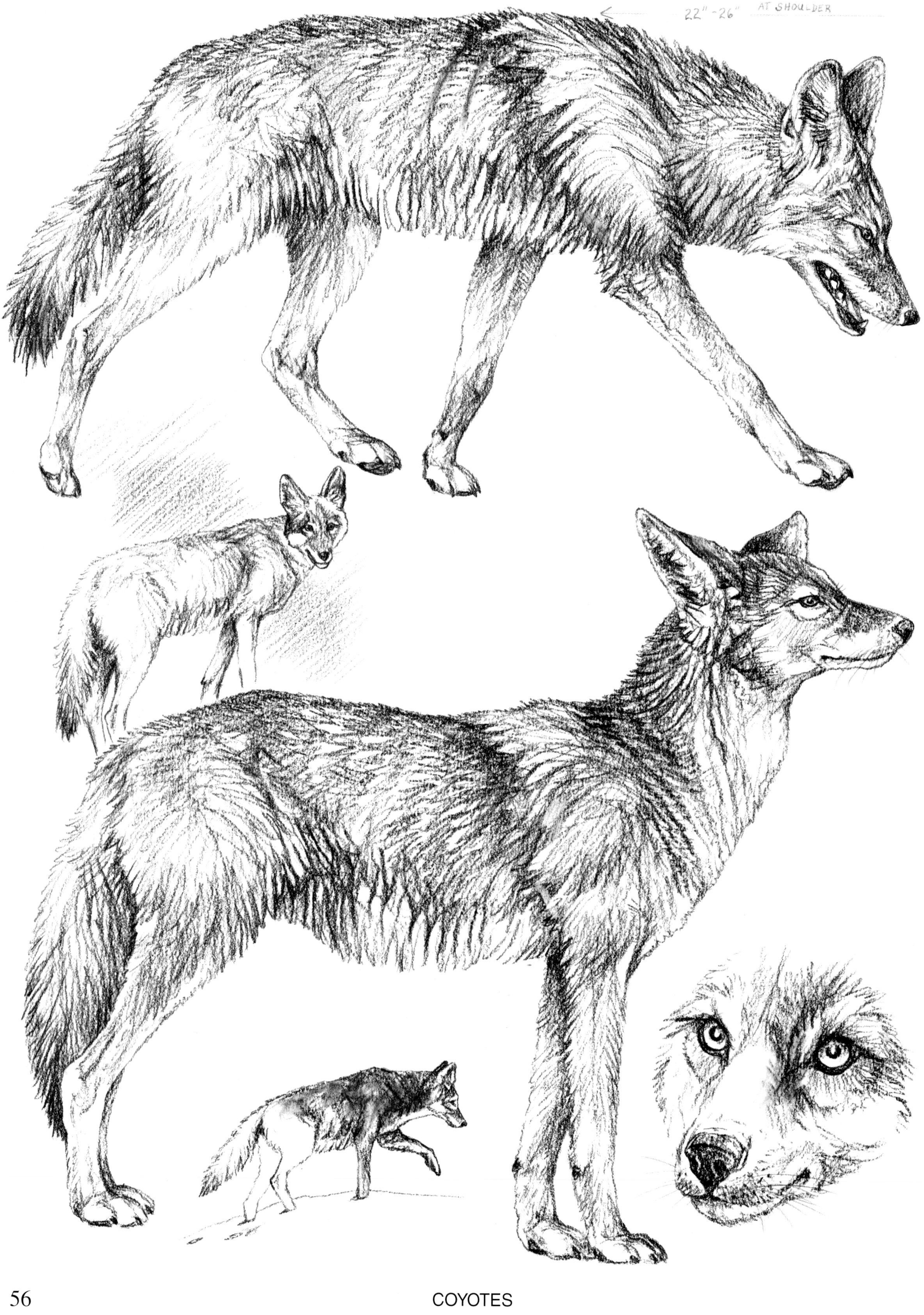
22"-26" AT SHOULDER

COYOTE / MALE (SEPTEMBER) 57

GRAY WOLF

The Gray wolf (Canis lupus) is a member of the Canidae family. Much larger than its coyote "brother", it weighs 75 - 125#'s on average. Males are larger than females. A wolf's coloration ranges from white to black, with gray being the most common shade. The more northern wolves are usually lighter colored than their southern counterparts. The bushy tailed (black tipped) predator stands about 36" at the shoulder and is 60" - 80" long.

A social animal, the Gray wolf lives in packs of 2 to 12 (usually 6 - 8), that is made up of parents, pups and relatives. The dominant male and female of the pack are called "alpha" and are the only ones that mate. A litter of (usually) 4 - 6 pups is born in a den in April/June. All members of the pack take a hand in raising the pups. The pack is a very defined and orderly group whereby all members know their "position" in the hierarchy.

The Gray wolf once roamed most of North America, but is now confined to Alaska, Canada, and the northern borders of the continental United States. It is now being reintroduced into areas where it once flourished but was eliminated. Controversy, of course, accompanies this; as ranchers and others are often opposed to having predators reestablished in areas where they can prey on livestock. Hopefully a suitable "balance" can be reached between nature and civilization and the wolf will regain his rightful "home" once again. Certain reintroductions of Gray and Mexican wolves has already resulted in shooting deaths of many of the animals.

Wolves are carnivores and their primary food is large mammals such as caribou, moose, and deer. A large pack will have a "home range" of 100 - 200 square miles to hunt, and often travel 30 miles a day in order to find prey. Hunting these large mammals is dangerous, and an injured wolf may be dispelled from the pack and left to hunt rodents, carrion, and fish on its own. Wolves usually live 10 - 15 years in the wild.

May the melodious "cry" of the Gray wolf continue to be heard reverberating across North America. It is truly a song that signifies freedom and wilderness.

ADULT MALE (AUGUST)

SNARLING
WOLF AT A MOOSE
KILL WITH 3 OTHER
WOLVES.

WINTER
COAT

GRAY WOLVES

60   GRAY WOLVES (TOP: SEPTEMBER, BOTTOM: JULY. COLORS RANGE FROM WHITE TO BLACK.

Wolf tracks / near Arctic Circle in Alaska

28"

Wolf Study (Alberta, Canada
* estimated at about 5,000 wolves in Alberta (1978)

Howling

62   GRAY WOLF / PUPS (JUNE)

PAW (FRONT) TRACK
Adult

4½"

GRAY WOLF / MALES

September/Alaska

TAIL
approx. 14-18"

Adult
Wolf Skull

GRAY WOLVES

64

MOUNTAIN LION

This big, tawny cat is North America's largest unspotted cat and is second only to the spotted Jaguar in size. It is characterized by its relatively small head and long, dark-tipped tail. Although it was once widely dispersed, it is now confined to the western part of North America from British Columbia south to Argentina. A few rare cats still survive in the Florida Everglades, but that is the only population east of the Mississippi river. The Mountain lion (Felis concolor) is also called cougar, panther and puma, depending on the region.

A mature male will weigh 150 - 200#'s on average and have a length of 8' - 9' (including 24" - 36" tail). It stands about 30" at the shoulder and is about one-third larger than the female. In the wild, they normally live 10 - 15 years.

The Mountain lion has no fixed breeding season, but the young are usually born in litters of 2 to 4 in the Spring/Summer season. Males are polygamous, breeding with any female in their area. Usually the mating pair stays together for a week or two before separating. The "kittens" are spotted and will remain near their rocky denning site until they are old enough to follow their mother on her hunting treks. They normally separate after a year or so. By then the young are full grown and have practiced and refined their hunting skills at their mothers side. Their main prey is deer (especially Mule deer) and the Mountain lion does most of its hunting by stalking near enough to its quarry to launch a speedy attack. A kill is usually made by biting into the back of the deers neck and twisting its head, thus breaking its spine or neck. The Mountain lion covers its uneaten food with leaves and vegetation and will return to eat from it until it begins to spoil.

Mountain lions are solitary creatures and each mature cat often travels 20 miles every day seeking prey. It, like other wildlife, has been encroached upon by development and more and more conflicts are occurring. Terrain that once housed healthy populations of predator and prey animals have now been claimed by homes and golf courses where the residents often feed and welcome the deer and elk (prey), and shoot and fear the predators (Mountain lions, coyotes, etc.) that come into "their space" to hunt.

Those of us who have explored wilderness areas and are lucky enough to see Mountain lions in their natural environment, will never forget the moments. The secretive, elusive cat is seldom seen. Also, if you have ever heard their bloodcurdling screams during mating, you will never forget that either. Sometimes, at night, ones tent seems very flimsy. A friend and fellow wildlife photographer died recently when a bear attacked him while he slept in his tent.

FEMALE (APRIL)

Retractable claws don't show in tracks.

Adult

Whiskers are white.

A few long white hairs above eye also.

Adult

Juvenile 9-10 months

30" (male)

Kitten 3-4 weeks. Blue eyes until at least 6 months old.

Male - average 175-200 lbs at maturity.

MOUNTAIN LIONS

Rounded ears

Spots are gone by 9-10 months.

* 7-8 MONTH OLD FEMALES (3 VIEWS)

2-3 week old. Dark spots.
Note - black back of ears
1 yd. at birth

Tail - 33-36" on adults.   Dark tip.

MOUNTAIN LIONS   67

Kitten

Cougars can run 35 MPH for a few hundred yards and leap more than 20 feet. A very efficient predator.

DARK-TIPPED TAIL

68

MOUNTAIN LIONS

Florida Panther / Female / estimated 100-125 lbs.
One of the world's most endangered animals!

Only 50-100 "pure"
Florida panthers exist.
(1999)

MALE

young female (no spots / probably 1 year old)
British Columbia, Canada

MOUNTAIN LIONS

Mountain lions are small headed cats.

Female
Study

MOUNTAIN LIONS / FEMALES & KITTEN

Retractable sharp claws
are protected in a sheath
until needed to "hook"
prey or a branch as this month old kitten is doing.

MOUNTAIN LION   / KITTEN (SEPTEMBER)   71

MOUNTAIN LION / MALE (AUGUST)

Kitten Study
September
California

Adult
Snow Track / 23" (Northern California '48

3" ROUND

TAIL DRAG MARK

73

PRONGHORN

The pronghorn (Antilocapra americana) is often misnamed "antelope", but is not related to members of that family. It is the only animal in the unique family, Antilocapra, and it sheds its horns yearly just as antlers are shed by deer. All other "horned" mammals in North America retain their horns and which grow longer every year. The pronghorn is the fastest mammal in North America and has been clocked at 70 mph for short periods. It has no natural enemies because of its speed, and only newborn fawns are vulnerable to bears, coyotes, and Golden eagles. Pronghorns are confined to the western half of the United States and range from southern Saskatchewan to Mexico, with Montana and Wyoming claiming the biggest populations. It is associated with the open plains and prairies where its phenomenal eyesight can detect movement and danger from miles away. When danger is detected, the pronghorn "flares" their long rump hair and thus alerts others nearby. Because they evolved on open, treeless country, they never developed the ability to jump vertically. That is why you'll see them crawl under fences, rather than jump over them.

Adult males (bucks) are about 36" - 40" at the shoulder, 4' - 5' long, and weigh (on average) 90 - 140#'s. Females (does) weigh 70 - 100#'s. This deer-like "speedster of the plains" is tan and white in color and the bucks have a black neck patch and facial marks. Both sexes sport horns; a does seldom exceeding 4" and a bucks peaking at about 20". The unique black horns are lyre-shaped and have short "prongs" that jut forward.

Mating occurs in September/October and fawns (commonly twins) are born during early summer. Newborns weigh about 4 pounds and are able to outrun enemies and keep up with adults in 6 or 7 days. Until then they are virtually odorless and spend a lot of time huddled in the grass. It is an interesting observation of nature to witness a doe give birth to one fawn and then move to another place to bear her second. This hereby separates the newborns and makes it less likely that a predator would discover both. Pronghorns normally live 8 to ten years in the wild.

　　　　　　　　　　　　　　BUCK (SEPTEMBER)

PRONGHORN / BUCK

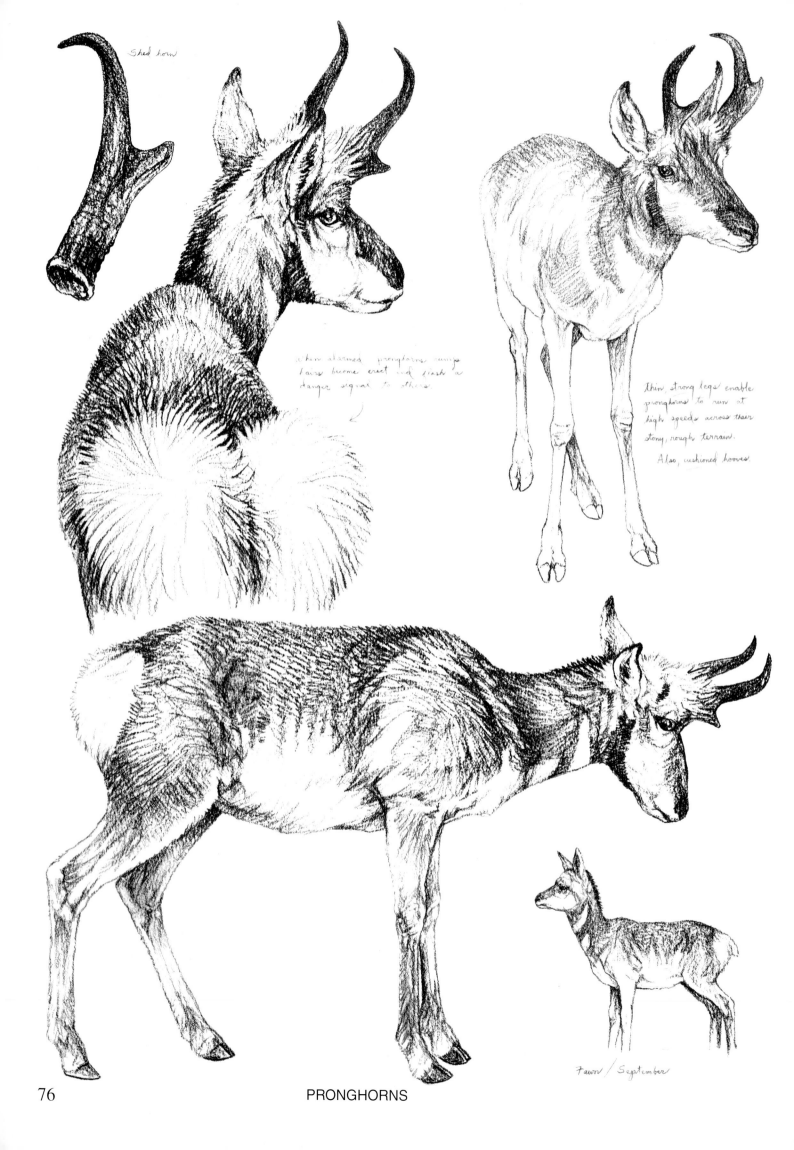

Shed horn

when alarmed pronghorns rump hairs become erect and flash a danger signal to others.

thin, strong legs enable pronghorns to run at high speeds across their stony, rough terrain.

Also, cushioned hooves.

Fawn / September

76   PRONGHORNS

When pronghorns run, they keep their mouths open wide, allowing them to inhale sufficient air. Its oversized heart and large lungs allow it to run long distances at high speeds without tiring. "Cruising" speed is about 40 mph, but 70 mph is obtainable for shorter spurts.

PRONGHORN / BUCKS

PRONGHORN / BUCKS (OCTOBER)

Pronghorn fawns are "odorless" for first few days — making them safer from predators.

Born: May/June

Pronghorns cannot jump fences (like deer) and usually crawl under rather than over them.

PRONGHORN / DOES & FAWN

Black mane

Newborn fawn/June
Wyoming

2½"

DOE
TRACK

80   PRONGHORN / DOES & FAWN

Buck track

3"

White blazes across tan neck

Pronghorn skull.
Horns are shed yearly.

PRONGHORN / BUCKS

"Pronged" buck horns.
Black, and 15-20" long
on mature adult
bucks.

Juvenile doe -
paler color than mature adults.

Doe horns - 2-4" long
with no prongs.

82

PRONGHORN / BUCK (SEPTEMBER)

BISON

The bison (Bison bison) is the largest terrestrial animal in North America and large males will weigh over 2,000#'s (females average 700 - 900#). A mature male will stand 6 feet at the shoulder and be 10 - 12 feet in length. The huge, bearded, shaggy maned, massive headed beast once roamed and migrated across a vast area of North America, but now mostly exists in National parks and private preserves. Small free-ranging herds do exist in a few areas such as Alaska, British Columbia and Northwest Territories. Wolves are really their only natural enemy nowadays and selected hunting is sometimes used to thin herds to keep them from overgrazing their habitat. Bison (also incorrectly called "buffalo") are dark brown in color, both sexes have upturned black horns, and are a grazing mammal that favors prairie grasses and sedges. During the frigid winters, their huge heads and wide hooves enable them to "plow" away the snow to reach the buried vegetation. Wild bison normally live about 25 years.

Bison mate in July/August, and the reddish-orange calves are born the following April/ May. Pregnant females (cows) usually separate from the herd during delivery and within a few days the calf is strong enough to run and keep up. The familiar "hump" of the bison begins to develop on the calves within three months. During the annual "rut" the huge breeding males (bulls) stage impressive fights between themselves. Charging one another with heads down, the mighty impact crash resonates across the plains. This battle continues until one finally flees. A herd bull will often mate with dozens of cows.

In centuries past, the bison numbered over 50 million strong and their thundering herds would stretch for miles and miles. By the early 1900's there were less than 1,000 bison surviving in the U.S. and Canada. It is heartening to see that bison numbers are improving due to conservation measures and protection. It would've been unforgivable to allow this noble and hardy "buffalo" to perish into extinction.

CALF (MAY)

Shaggy appearance!
Shedding winter coat

Cows & calf (nursing) / May

Nose

Winter coat

BISON / COWS & CALF

Reddish-orange colored coat
at birth.

Early study
April

Calves are less than
2 weeks old.

Approximately 70-75 pounds

BISON CALVES

cow horns curve inward more
than bull horns.

Delta Junction, Alaska
is a good "viewing" area
for bison.

Cows horns are smaller
than bulls.

May 25

Calf — 1-2 weeks
Reddish brown color

Cow

BISON / COWS & CALF

6 feet at shoulder

Tail - 2-3 ft long

5"

TRACKS

88

BISON / BULLS

Beard 8-10" long

Yearling bull / July

Bull horns are about 18" long and 12" in circumference on mature animals.

BISON / BULLS

BISON / BULL

TOP: BISON CALF (7 months); COW (ADULT)   BOTTOM: BISON BULL (SEPTEMBER)   91

Cows / Summer coat

beginning
horns

Calf / 3 months old
July

BISON / COWS & CALF

MOUNTAIN GOAT

The Mountain goat (Oreamnos americanus) is not a true goat and has no relatives in North America. Whereas a "true" goat's horns sweep up and curve back (and are "ridged"), the Mountain goat's horns are relatively smooth and curve back only slightly. North America's "goat" is white and has a black nose, horns, eyes, and hooves. It is a hardy, sure-footed creature who dwells in high mountain terrain of northwestern North America, and has natural populations from Idaho to Alaska. They are often confused with the Dall sheep who they often share ranges with; however, their black horns, longer hair, and "beard" should distinguish them. Although the Mountain goat males are larger, both sexes are similar in appearance (even horns are similar in length, but the females (nannies) are more slender). A mature male (billy) will weigh around 200#'s, stands 40" - 48" at the shoulder, and is 5' - 6' long.

Mating occurs in November/December, and the normally segregated males join the groups of females (and immatures) to breed. Billies do not collect harems of nannies and there doesn't seem to be the "rutting battles" that often accompany other species. Young (kids) are born the following May/June, and will stay near their mother until the next mating season. Mountain goats live in dangerous terrain but have few natural enemies besides the Golden eagle. Their lifespan is about 15 years in the wild.

Mountain goats are slow-paced animals. This may be due to their rugged, rocky terrain, or the fact that few predators pursue them. Goats are most active during the morning hours and their diet consists of grasses, mosses, lichens and brushy material. Most goats migrate from their high summer environment to lower (below treeline) terrain during the snowy winters. It is there where they are most vulnerable to predators such as Mountain lions and wolves, but their excellent eyesight and rubbery-soled hooves usually provide salvation.

BILLY (SEPTEMBER)

Young
Billy /September

September/Kid

JUNE

MOUNTAIN GOATS

MOUNTAIN GOAT / BILLY

MOUNTAIN GOAT / NANNY & KID (SEPTEMBER)

November

KID
3 months old

16"

Jasper National Park, Canada
Billy
September

3-3½"

MOUNTAIN GOATS

36" - 40" at shoulder

Nannies (female) horns are as long as a
Billies (male) horns, but are usually more
slender. A mature goats horns are about
8-11" on average.

Front hooves
3" x 2½"

98   MOUNTAIN GOAT / NANNIES

MOUNTAIN GOAT / BILLY (OCTOBER)

MUSKOX

The muskox (Ovibos moschatus) is a unique animal of the North. This stocky, longhaired animal is called "omingmak" by the Eskimos, and taxonomists classify it with the goats and sheep. The muskox has a dark brown coat with a light colored "saddle" on its back, whitish lower legs and cloven hooves. A mature male (bull) weighs 600 - 900#'s, stands approximately 60" at the shoulder, and is 7' - 8' long. Females (cows) are one-third smaller. Both sexes have horns.

Mating occurs from August/October, and young (calves) are born the following Spring (weighing about 25#'s). During the annual "rut" the bulls put on spectacular battles, trying to win the right to breed with the herds females. Competing bulls will charge one another at full speed and collide on their horn bosses (6" of horn and bone over the impact area protect their brains). These collisions are repeated over and over until one bull submits and leaves the area. The "crack" of smashing horns carries for miles across the northern tundra.

The range and numbers of Muskox are very limited due mainly to overhunting in the past. Their "defense position" of banding together with their heads facing the predator (and their vulnerable calves behind them) proved effective against wolves but was futile against men armed with rifles. Often times whole herds were shot. Muskox are now found free-ranging in Alaska and the Northwest Territories. Reintroduction into other former ranges is being considered. Their summer diet consists of green grasses and willows, and (because of the heavy snow cover) must survive on woody plants during the long winters.

Although it lives in seemingly barren and unforgiving country, the hardy muskox will thrive and expand its numbers if given the space and isolation it requires.

MUSKOX / BULL (AUGUST)

Calves / June
Estimated 50 pds.

Dominant herd
bull
June
Estimated 800 pds.

MUSKOX / BULL & CALVES

MUSKOX / BULL (MAY)

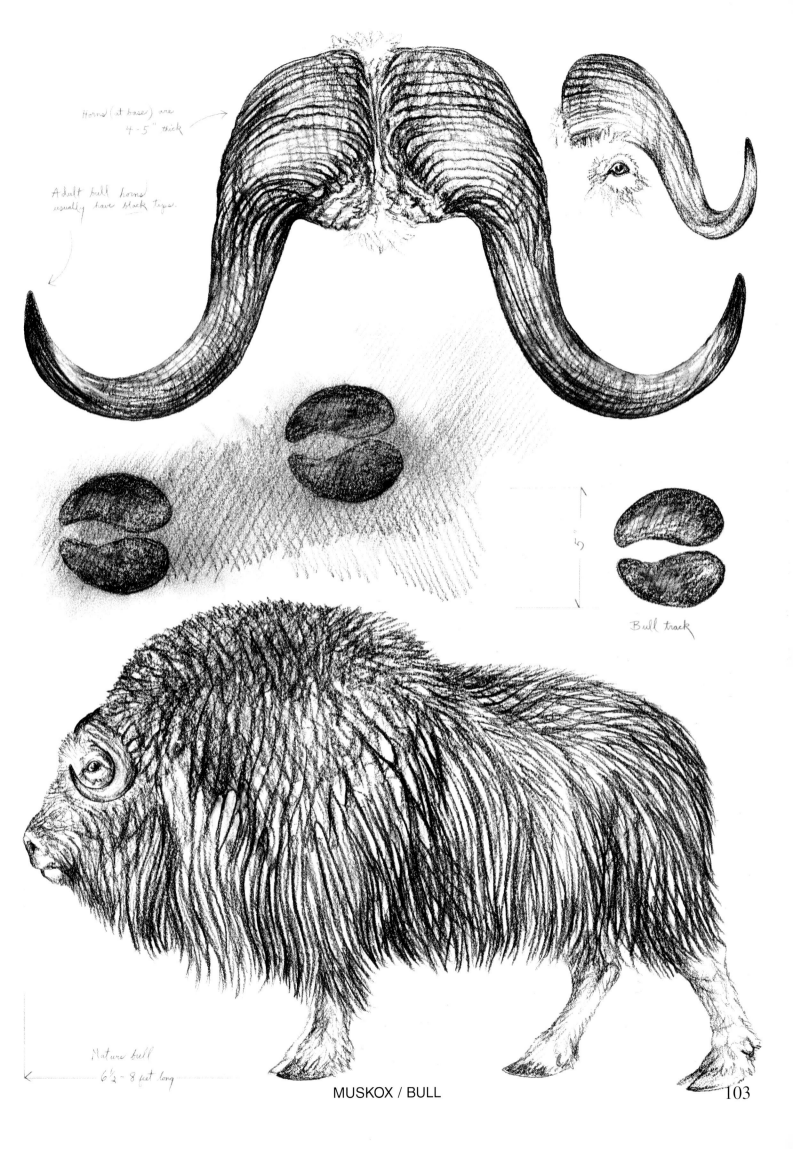

Horns (at base) are
4-5" thick

Adult bull horns
usually have black tips.

5"

Bull track

Mature bull

6½ - 8 feet long

MUSKOX / BULL

104   MUSKOX / BULLS   (DECEMBER)

Newborn
April

Calf
May

Cow
May
Alaska

MUSKOX / COW & CALVES

BIGHORN SHEEP

The Bighorn sheep (Ovis canadensis) is a member of the family Bovidae, which means it is cloven hooved, has hollow horns, and is a cud-chewer. It inhabits high, rocky areas and ranges from southern British Columbia and Alberta south into Mexico. In my drawings and photographs, I separated them by calling the northern bighorns "Rocky Mountain bighorns" and the more southern bighorns "Desert bighorns". They are the same specie but their appearance and habits are different due to their differing environments.

Bighorn males (rams) are distinguished by their massive curled horns, whereas the females (ewes) have shorter, straighter horns. A mature northern bighorn ram will weigh up to 300#'s, while his desert counterpart normally peaks at about 200#'s. Ewes will average 125 - 175#'s. Bighorns stand 36" - 42" at the shoulder and are 5' - 6' long. Their color ranges from dark brown (in the north) to pale buff (in the desert). Their muzzle, belly, back of legs, and rump are white, and they have a brown tail and a pale ring around the eyes.

Mating season normally peaks in November/December, but the Desert bighorns often breed earlier and the battles between competing males are less combative. During early autumn the rams begin "testing" one another with head-butting and these skirmishes slowly evolve into spectacular 20 mph "crashes" into one another. Usually only rams with similar sized horns will fight to determine dominance. Large, heavily-horned rams may go unchallenged. Bighorn horns are normally more massive and less flared than those of the Dall/Stone specie. Also, their horns are more frequently "broomed" in order for them to see to the side better (and, of course, due to falls or battles). During May/June (and earlier in the desert) the pregnant ewes seek out safe quarters in the cliffs to bear their young (lambs). After the mating season, the rams again band together and separate from the ewes, lambs, and immatures. Life span is about 12 - 15 years in the wild.

Because of their rugged terrain, the Bighorn sheep have an advantage over predators, but Mountain lions, Golden eagles, and wolves still take a significant toll. Their summer diet consists mainly of grasses and sedges, and in winter (in the north) they must switch to woody plants and brush.

LAMB (SEPTEMBER)

Ewes' horns rarely exceed
12 inches

EWE
TRACK

2½"

During the autumn "rut" rams will determine an ewe's breeding receptivity by scent. A ram will hold his head high, curl his upper lip, and the ewe's odor is evaluated.

3½"

Ram track

　　　ROCKY MOUNTAIN BIGHORN / RAMS

SHOULDER HEIGHT 38-42" RAM

WHITE RUMP SHORT BLACK TAIL

WHITE MUZZLE

Bighorns have more tightly curled horns than Dall or Stone sheep.

ROCKY MOUNTAIN BIGHORN / RAMS

Old ram
Winter coat

Colt match at
10-11 years

Maximum life span is
about 15. Predators,
injuries & poor supplies
limit population explosions.

Bighorns (with subspecies) range
from Canada to Mexico.

20-30 yr
horns

RAM
TRACKS

FULL
CURL

Broomed
horns
Tips broken off

Ewe & lambs July

Bighorn
Lamb September
Yearling

BIGHORN
LAMB AT BIRTH:

10" HIGH AT SHOULDER
8-9 POUNDS
TWINS ARE RARE

Rams / August / Wyoming

Largest of North American Sheep
Rams 250-300 #'s

"BROOMED" HORNS
NOVEMBER

ANNUAL
GROWTH
RINGS

RAMS
SUMMER
COAT

112

ROCKY MOUNTAIN BIGHORN / RAMS

ROCKY MOUNTAIN RAMS

114   DESERT BIGHORN / RAM (SEPTEMBER)

36"
at shoulder

Desert Bighorns are smaller than the
northern Rocky Mountain Bighorns. Mature rams
weigh about 175-190 pounds.

DESERT BIGHORN / RAMS

115

Desert bighorns are the least populous of North American wild sheep and, because of the open, arid country they inhabit, have few predators. They have remarkable stamina and often go for a week without water (except for that acquired by eating cactus, etc.). Their tawny, buff coat helps them blend in with their environment.

Horns (unlike antlers) are not shed yearly.

DESERT BIGHORN / EWE

2¼"

DESERT EWE TRACK

Ewes are approximately ¼ smaller than rams.

Also, Desert Bighorns are lighter colored than the northern Rocky Mountain Bighorns.

Ewes / August

Mature ewe's weigh 125 - 150 pounds.

Beginning Horns
August

DESERT BIGHORN / EWES & LAMB
117

DESERT BIGHORN / EWE (MARCH)

BLACK TAIL

DESERT BIGHORN / RAMS   119

15"

RAM
TRACKS

DESERT BIGHORN / RAMS

DALL SHEEP

The Dall sheep (Ovis dalli dalli) is the white sheep of Alaska. It is the smallest of North American sheep and a mature male (ram) weighs 175 - 225#'s. Females (ewes) weigh, on average, 120 - 150#'s. The rams sport yellowish, wide-flaring horns, while the ewes have short, straighter horns that seldom exceed 12". Because the wide flare allows better sideways vision, the rams seldom "broom" their horn tips as is common with the Bighorn sheep. Different areas of Alaska seem to have different horn configurations; some more flared than the more tight curls of other regions. A mature ram is 36" - 40" high at the shoulder and is approximately 5' long. Because, perhaps, I have spent so much time in the mountains with these beautiful and magnificent creatures, they have become my "favorite". To behold a full-curled autumn ram silhouetted against a blue sky is a memorable scene. A "full-curl", incidentally, occurs in about 7 or 8 years. Most sheep don't live over 12 years in the wild.

Dall sheep inhabit high alpine meadows and steep sloped terrain. They have excellent vision, and if danger arises they escape to the rocky crags above. Wolves are its main predator, but occasionally a Golden eagle, wolverine, or lynx claims a lamb or injured/sick adult. The diet of Dall sheep is limited and consists of grasses, sedges, brush and lichens. Severe winters and springs can claim many sheep by making food unavailable or difficult.

Mating occurs in November/December and the young (lambs) are born in May/June on a secluded rocky cliff. The frisky, snow-white lambs are able to run within a few days and often spend their first summer frolicking and drinking their mothers rich milk. If there is a ram that is much larger than the others, he will often intimidate the smaller rams into not challenging him. Otherwise the rams will challenge and battle one another until a victor emerges. It is natures way of passing on the genetics of the strongest and healthiest to the upcoming generation.

LAMB (JUNE)

Nursing Lamb
June

Ewe & Lamb Study

DALL SHEEP / LAMBS

tracks

DALL SHEEP/EWE (MAY)

Ewes / Summer

DALL SHEEP / EWES

SUMMER COAT

WINTER COAT

SOFT PAD

HARD OUTER EDGE

FRONT HOOVES

Front Foot

DALL SHEEP / RAMS

Dall Rams
Alaska Range
Alaska

DALL SHEEP / RAMS

3"

TRACK

128

DALL SHEEP / RAMS

DALL SHEEP / RAM (SEPTEMBER)

STONE SHEEP

The Stone sheep (Ovis dalli stonei) is a subspecie of the all-white Dall. It ranges from the Yukon south to British Columbia's Stikine river. It is slightly larger than the Dall and its blue-black coloration pattern is that of the bighorn; that is, its dark body is contrasted by its white rump and belly, and the white edging running down the rear of its legs. It also has some white on its face and the horns of the males (rams) are normally heavier than those of the Dall. In between the more northern Dall and the more southern Stone are sheep with characteristics of both.

Rams usually weigh over 200#'s at maturity and stand 38" - 40" at the shoulder. They are about 5' long, have black hooves and amber-colored, flaring horns. (Incidentally, the longest set of horns ever recorded on any North American sheep belongs to a Stone; both horns are over 50" long and have a base circumference of 15".) Females (ewes) are just as colorful as males but are smaller (150#'s). They bear their first young (lamb) at age 3, and have a single lamb every year after. The mating season is November/December and the lambs are born May/June of the following year in a secluded, rocky area. During this rutting season, the rams must battle one another to determine who will sire the next generation. These battles are frequent and during the "fights" the two opposing foes will separate, and then, after rearing on their hind legs, drop and charge. The collision is intense and broken horns and noses are the result of not making exact contact. After about a month, all the eligible ewes are mated, and the rams band together and separate from the others. They'll normally stay separated until the following October, unless the restrictions of winter food again reunites them on windswept slopes.

Grazing animals, the Stone sheep feed on the grasses of the alpine meadows. In areas where predators (such as wolves) are scarce, the sheep will feed low in the valleys where food is plentiful. Stone sheep usually live about 12 years, but those that reach 14 or 15 are the "trophy" animals that hunters, artists, and photographers relish. An excellent place to see "Stones" is along the "Alcan highway".

Horns of the Stone rams are normally heavier than those of the more-northern Dall rams.

STONE SHEEP / RAM

131

STONE SHEEP / RAMS

STONE SHEEP / RAM (APRIL)

STONE SHEEP / RAM (AUGUST)

Ewes must sometimes use their sharp horns to protect their lambs from predators.

Lambs are usually born on secluded, rugged cliffs and are weaned within 2 months.

Summer coat

Matures ewes weigh around 150 pounds

Winter coat
November

STONE SHEEP / EWES

135

Black tail
White rump-belly
Whitish face

Approximately
12" horns

Young Ewe – Spring coat
April

136   STONE SHEEP / EWES

CARIBOU

The caribou (Rangifer tarandus) is a large, stout member of the deer family and is usually associated with the northern tundra areas of North America. Caribou are generally brown with a white belly, rump and neck. Their shaggy, tannish-colored summer coats give way to the splendid rich coats of autumn. Both males (bulls) and females (cows) have antlers, but the cows are relatively small and spindly compared to the magnificent long, palmated antlers of the mature bulls. Weights vary widely, but a mature bull will average 275 - 400#'s, stand 45" - 55" at the shoulder, and be 5' long. (Large bulls of Alaska's Aleutian Islands will often weigh over 700#'s.) Females are 175 - 225#'s.

All caribou (and reindeer) throughout the world are considered to be the same specie. Subspecies are: the Barren-ground, the Woodland, and the Mountain caribou. All have distinguishing characteristics, but are generally similar in appearance. Alaska has only the Barren-ground, while Canada, Greenland, Labrador, and Newfoundland have a variety of subspecies. Very few caribou are found south of the Canadian border. The caribou is a migratory animal that must keep moving in order to find adequate food. Summer vegetation (willows, grasses, and plants) is plentiful and the caribou are able to put on fat-reserves that will help sustain them through the long arctic winters; where they must survive on a meager diet of lichens and reindeer moss.

The bulls lose the "velvet" of their antlers in August/September, and the mating season will usually be over by November. During the spring (May/June) the caribou cows migrate to their particular "calving grounds" to bear a single "calf". The calves are able to keep up with the moving herd within a few days. Also, during this period, the wolf (who usually accompany the migrating herds) preys heavily on the newborns in order to sustain the ravenous appetites of their own young. Perhaps because of the protection it affords them, the cows retain their antlers until after their calves are born.

The caribou has large, concave hoofs which support the animal in soft ground and in snow. It is also an excellent swimmer and is able to swim wide, icey rivers swiftly and easily. The domesticated caribou, the reindeer, is an important animal to many northern people who need it to survive. Also, when wild caribou change their normal migration routes, many of the Native people (who rely upon it for their food and clothing) are faced with hardships. A wild caribou normally lives 10 - 12 years.

BARREN-GROUND CARIBOU / BULL (SEPTEMBER)

STRIDE 16"–18"

"Velvet" covered antlers
August

Denali Nat'l.
Park,
Alaska

138   BARREN-GROUND CARIBOU / BULLS

BARREN-GROUND CARIBOU / IN "VELVET" (AUGUST)   139

Calf / May

BARREN-GROUND CARIBOU

BARREN-GROUND CARIBOU / BULL (SEPTEMBER)

"Velvet" is usually shed in August/September

Mature Bull 4½'–5' at shoulder.

BULL TRACK IN MUD

5"

Antler formation varies greatly
These 3 bulls were sketched in September
at Denali National Park, Alaska.

BARREN-GROUND CARIBOU / BULLS

143

COW TRACKS

144 WOODLAND CARIBOU / COWS

young cow

Bulls
October
coat

WOODLAND CARIBOU

Cow antlers are shed April-June

Cow / April

Yearling / April

Antlers

Calf / May
(about 25 pounds)

WOODLAND CARIBOU / COW & CALVES

BLACK-TAILED DEER

The Sitka black-tailed deer (Odocoileus hemionus sitkensis) is the deer of the Alaskan rain forests and the northern coast of British Columbia. It is smaller than other blacktails and has a shorter-face. They have a typical blacktail antler branching, with three points (including the eyeguard tine) on each side. A mature male (buck) weighs about 110 - 150#'s, stands 36" - 38" at the shoulder, and is about 5' long. Females (does) average 75 - 95#'s. The blacktails coloration resembles that of a whitetails but has a dark horseshoe-shaped mark on its forehead. The blacktails tail is black on the top and white underneath.

Mating season is October/November and the 5# "fawns" are born the following May/June. They, like other deer and elk fawns, are born with a camouflaged "spotted" brown coat, and they spend much of the first few weeks hidden in the grass. Soon, however, the rich milk of nursing has given them the strength to stay at their mothers side and to escape most predators. Although predators such as the wolf and bear take a certain percentage of the fawns and adults, the main cause of population declines is severe winters and the loss of quality winter range due to clearcut logging.

During summer the blacktails feed on the plentiful herbaceous vegetation and shrubs, but during the winter they are often reduced to surviving on evergreens and woody browse. A wild Sitka black-tailed deer seldom lives past 10 - 12 years.

The other North American blacktail subspecie, the Columbian blacktail (Odocoileus hemionus columbianus), ranges from the British Columbia coast south along the western coasts of Washington, Oregon, and California. They are not as short-faced as the Sitka, and are generally larger. Their main predator is the Mountain lion who flourishes through these regions.

SITKA BLACK-TAILED DEER / FAWN (JUNE)

"VELVET"
August

Large buck
October

Front foot

White patch

SITKA BLACK-TAILED DEER / BUCKS

Non-typical antlers

3 points (including eyeguard)
is most typical Black-tailed
antler branching.

September

SITKA BLACK-TAILED DEER / BUCKS

149

Row of spots on each side of spine.

August
(spots gone)

June
2-3 weeks old

July

June

SITKA BLACK-TAILED DEER

Fawn / July
Alaska

152   SITKA BLACK-TAILED DEER (AUGUST)

2½"

November

Running track
2-5 feet

July "in velvet"

SITKA BLACK-TAILED DEER / BUCKS

153

Mature does / 80 pd. average

does, in prime (5-9) bear twins.

does / Summer

COLUMBIAN BLACK-TAILED DEER (FAWN AND DOE)

MULE DEER

The Mule deer (Odocoileus hemionus) inhabits the prairies, hills, and open spaces of the Rocky Mountain region from Alberta to Mexico. Colorado, California, Oregon, Montana and Wyoming have the largest populations. Also, the Blacktail deer is considered a subspecie of the Mule deer, but because of their different characteristics, I will separate the two here in my writing, art, and photographs. The big-eared "Mulie" prefers rough, mountainous country as opposed to the more wooded terrain of the Whitetail.

A mature male Mule deer (buck) is a stocky animal that stands 42" high at the shoulder, is over 6' long, and averages 175 - 250#'s in weight. Its antlers differ from the Whitetails in that each antler beam forks twice, forming long, straight points. Also, the Mule deer's antlers often lack the brow tines that are often very prominent on a Whitetail rack. Deer are normally a reddish-brown during the summer and turn a more grayish color in winter. Other characteristics include a round, black-tipped tail, creamy-white belly, and white throat patches, rump, and insides of legs and ears. Females (does) have no antlers and weigh 100 - 150#'s.

Mule deer usually migrate between summer and winter ranges. They seem to prefer early morning and late afternoon feeding, and often retire to shady, protected areas for the mid-day. However, during nighttime, they more likely will "bed" in the open. Their diet consists mainly of grasses during the summer months and brush and browse during the winter. They, unlike other large mammals, don't "paw" through the snow to reach the frozen grasses. All deer have an excellent sense of smell but their eyesight does not seem to detect stationary objects that may be a threat. Main predators are the Mountain lion (a mature cat will kill 2 or 3 Mule deer every 10 days) and (in the more northern areas) the wolf. Normally 10 years is the life span of a wild Mule deer.

Most mating has occurred by December and the young "fawns" are born the following summer. Most weigh about 6#'s, are "spotted", and nurse from their mother until winter. By then they have lost their camouflaged spotted coat and become independent. Does will breed when they are 1 1/2 years old. After the initial "single" fawn, twins are most common.

156   BUCK (OCTOBER)

Shed antler -
March

Estimated
40" at shoulder

Young buck Study - Alberta

MULE DEER / BUCKS

Doe ears – 8"-9" long
and about 5" wide.

Walking track / Doe

MULE DEER / DOES

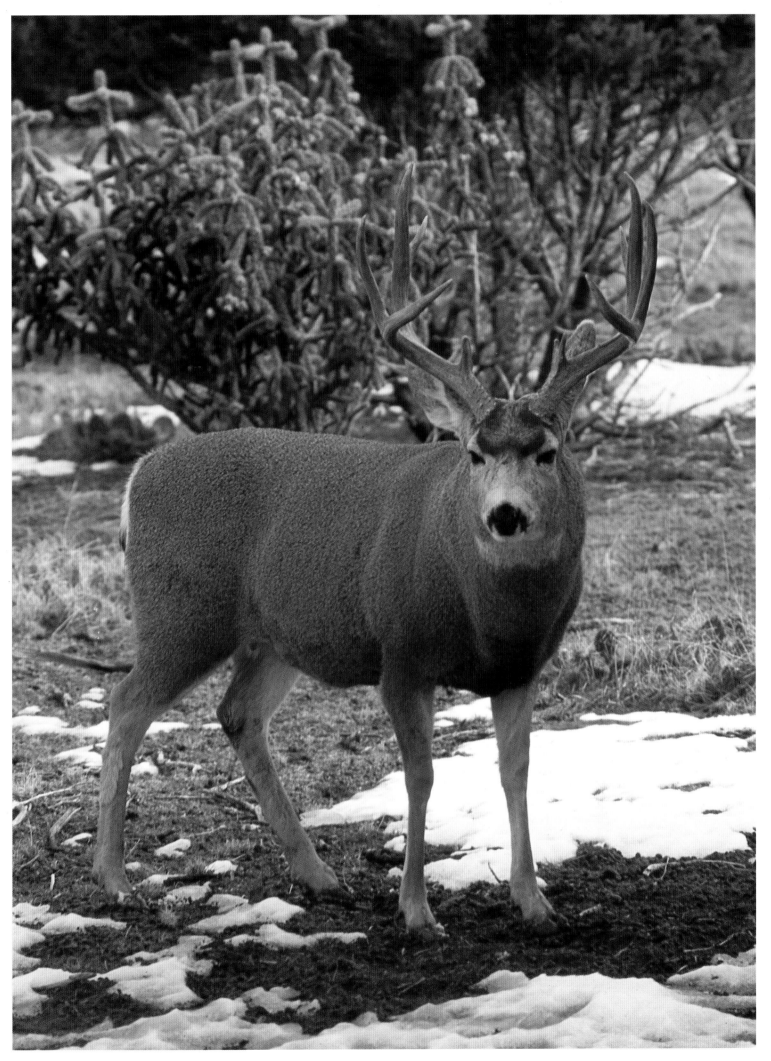

MULE DEER / BUCK (JANUARY) 159

160

MULE DEER / BUCKS

In "velvet"
August / Yukon territory, Canada

10"-11"
Adult ear length.

20-22"
stride

3¼"
Buck

Typical -
Each main beam forks twice.

Yearling
"Spike" buck

MULE DEER / BUCKS

Mule deer fawns weigh about 6 #'s at birth and their spotted coat is duller than a whitetails. Its voice is a "blat" or "bawl". Mountain lions, wolves, and bears are main predators.

162   MULE DEER / FAWN

MULE DEER/BUCK (JANUARY)

MULE DEER / BUCKS

40"-42"

TAIL
White, cylindrical, with
2" black tip.

Short brow lines

Buck Study
New Mexico

MULE DEER / BUCKS

WHITETAIL DEER

The Whitetail deer (Odocoileus vIrginianus) is the most plentiful big-game mammal in North America. It is native to North America and, because of its adaptability, has flourished in modern times; despite the elimination of much of its original territory. Estimates state that the 500,000 whitetails of 1900 have grown to over 19,000,000 in 1999. Whitetails range over much of the United States (except the West's driest areas) and the southern parts of Canada. It has various subspecies, and ranges in size from the large northern deer to the tiny Florida Key deer. Weights for mature northern males (bucks) is 150 - 225#'s on average, and usually less than 90#'s for the Key whitetail. Shoulder height for the large deer is 38" - 42", with a 5' - 6' length. Despite regional differences, whitetails are basically similar in coloration. Brownish-gray coats with a white belly, throat patches, and chin. Its black nose is offset with white and the dark eyes are circled in white. Its coat changes from the brownish-gray of autumn/winter to a reddish tinge during the summer months. Its antlers consist of a main beam from which numerous tines grow upwards from; they do not "fork" like those of the mule/blacktail specie. When alarmed, a whitetail will "flash" his large tail, exposing the white underpart,

Whitetails have a wide range of foods throughout its vast range, ranging from apples and acorns to twigs and grasses. Whitetails also frequent corn fields, grain fields, and vegetable gardens. During September the bucks lose their antler "velvet" and by October their necks begin to swell for the "rut" which occurs until December. After the females (does) are bred, the bucks will shed their antlers (usually by January) and not begin to regrow them until late spring. "Fawns" are born May/June in most regions. Although the whitetail has many wildlife predators, the main reason for whitetail deaths (besides severe weather and food shortage) is their harassment by dogs. Often times packs of "pets" will literally run down and kill (or cause to die) every deer in an area. Whitetails normally live 10 - 12 years in the wild.

BUCK "IN VELVET" (SEPTEMBER)

"8 pointer"

white patch

WHITETAIL DEER / BUCKS

Black-brown tail may be over a foot long. When alarmed,
the deer raises its tail to flash the white underside.

Mature doe —
32" - 36" at shoulder

Doe track

168   WHITETAIL DEER / DOES

Buck track –
toes spread apart
when running.

3"

3 views
Young buck in "velvet" / September

Study

British Columbia,
Canada

WHITETAIL DEER "IN VELVET" / BUCKS

169

ANTLERS

By September (in most areas) a buck's antlers are grown and hardened, and the dried "velvet" peels away shortly thereafter. Antlers are shed after the "rut" and new antlers begin to grow the following spring.

TRACKS

WHITETAIL DEER / BUCKS

Front hoof

Fawns / Summer

WHITETAIL DEER / FAWNS

"Southern" Whitetail

Non-typical rack / Autumn

172   WHITETAIL DEER / BUCK (OCTOBER)

Fawn "spots" are random, except for 2 straight lines of spots along back.

Brown eyes with black pupils.

Metatarsal gland

Autumn "rut"
(Swelled neck)

est. 28"

Ear spread
16"-19"

Mature Buck
38-40" at shoulder

Stride
about 18"

"Spike" buck

WHITETAIL DEER / BUCKS

WHITETAIL DEER / BUCK (NOVEMBER)

Whitetail deer are a very adaptable specie that can reside and flourish near human habitation if food and cover are adequate.

In 1900 there were less the 500,000 whitetails in the United States. Now, 100 years later, there are over 19,000,000.

176

Buck track

"Button" buck

November

28" at shoulder / Mature buck.

FLORIDA "KEY" DEER / BUCKS

178   FLORIDA "KEY" DEER / BUCK (NOVEMBER)

FLORIDA "KEY" DEER / DOE (NOVEMBER)

180   FLORIDA "KEY" DEER / DOES

WHITETAIL BUCK / COUES SPECIE (ARIZONA)

This whitetail deer is found in Mexico and southern Arizona. It is a small deer with bucks seldom weighing over 100 pounds and does weighing about 65 pounds. It is often referred to locally as "Sonora whitetail" or "Arizona whitetail".

181

ROCKY MOUNTAIN ELK

Rocky Mountain elk (Cervus canadensis nelsoni) range from British Columbia, Alberta, and Saskatchewan south through the Rocky Mountain states. It is also being reintroduced into various other locations in North America. Adult Rocky Mountain males (bulls) will normally weigh about 700 - 800#'s, and mature females (cows) about 500#'s. The shoulder height of bulls is about 5' and they are 8' - 9' long. They have brown coats with dark brown heads and necks, blackish belly and legs, and a whitish rump. They are slightly smaller and lighter-colored than the less numerous Roosevelt elk of the Pacific Northwest.

Bulls sport long, majestic, wide-spreading antlers, and during the autumn "rut" will use these impressive "racks" to either battle or intimidate other area bulls. September is the time when "velvet" is shed, necks are swollen, "bugles" echo across the hills and valleys, and herd bulls gather harems of cows. The mating season is normally complete by November, and the bulls become more tolerant of one another and begin to feed heartily in order to replenish their strength. Spotted "calves" are born May/June and weigh about 30#'s. Elk cows "hide" their newborn calves in cover until they are strong enough to join the herd. Sometimes one cow will "babysit" the herds calves while the others feed. This sharing of duties allows each cow time to feed undisturbed. An elks diet consists mostly of grasses, but it also browses on other vegetation. Sometimes elk are fed during the winter months, as is done at a refuge near Jackson Hole, Wyoming.

Elk, when undisturbed by man or predators, prefer to feed in early morning and late afternoon. This is usually a time of "poor light" for photographers, but by using fast film (and tripod) you can usually get suitable reference photo's. The mating season, however, is the time to concentrate your efforts, as the elk are less "shy" and are in their prime coats and antlers. Rocky Mountain elk usually live about 15 years in the wild. Mountain lions, wolves, and bears take occasional elk, but the adults are formidable "foes" and so only young, sick, or injured animals are normally preyed upon successfully.

182   CALF (JULY)

Antlers are normally shed by March.
New antlers begin in April.

"VELVET" / August

Bull / January

ROCKY MOUNTAIN ELK / BULLS

183

5 feet

Prime bull antlers

Prime bulls usually have 5-7 points.
A seventh point is called an "imperial" point

(4th)
Largest
tine

Brow
tines

9 feet long (bulls)

ROCKY MOUNTAIN ELK / BULLS

5 ft. high at shoulder

October
"IN RUT"

Bulls are very aggressive during this mating season that runs September/October.

ROCKY MOUNTAIN ELK / BULLS

Calves
Summer

> Mature cow
7 ft. in length

Cow / August

COW
TRACKS

TOP: ROCKY MOUNTAIN ELK / BULLS "SPARRING" (DECEMBER)
BOTTOM: ROCKY MOUNTAIN ELK / COW (JULY)

187

ROCKY MOUNTAIN ELK / BULL (JUNE)

ROCKY MOUNTAIN ELK / BULL (SEPTEMBER)

"Rutting"
Bull Study
Jasper National Park
Alberta, Canada
September

ROCKY MOUNTAIN ELK / BULLS

"Bugle" / September

Bulls / July

ROCKY MOUNTAIN ELK / BULLS

191

ROOSEVELT ELK

The Roosevelt elk (Cervus canadensis roosevelti) is found scattered about the Pacific Northwest. It is larger, darker colored, and sports more massive antlers than do the Rocky Mountain elk that are found east of the Cascade mountains in the United States and Canada. Large males (bulls) on Alaska's Afognak Island will often weigh over 1300#'s, but a more average weight is 700 - 900#'s. Adult females (cows) normally weigh around 500 - 600#'s. Elk cows (unlike caribou cows) don't grow antlers, but a bull elk in its prime may don magnificent antlers over 5' long. Large bulls stand 5' at the shoulder and are 9' - 10' long. Roosevelt elk have brown bodies and dark brown heads and necks. The belly and legs are almost black and it has a whitish-yellow rump. During the summer months the elks coat lightens to almost tan.

The elk, or wapiti (as the Shawnee Indians called it), has recently been reintroduced into various areas of North America and seems to be thriving and multiplying. In fact, a recent survey estimated that the 40,000 elk of the early 1900's has grown to over 800,000 today. It is truly a wildlife success story. Elk are hardy eaters and their diet ranges from grazing foods to browsing vegetation. Elk, like deer, often overeat their range if they become too populous, and are then subject to massive starvation. Most governments have departments of Fish & Game that monitor these situations. Mountain lions, wolves, and bears are occasional predators. Fifteen years is an average life span for a Roosevelt elk.

The mating season begins in September and it is then that the bulls eery, high pitched "bugle" resonates across the meadows and through the timber; trumpeting a challenge or warning to all other bulls. By late October the fighting and mating is complete and the elk disperse to their wintering grounds. The spotted "calves" are born the following May/June, when mild weather and plentiful food increases their survival odds.

ROOSEVELT ELK / COW (APRIL)

Spike bull - July

mid-August

September

ROOSEVELT ELK / BULLS

Roosevelt elk are bigger, darker in color and
their antlers are shorter and less symmetrical
than the Rocky Mountain specie.

32" - 35"
Bull stride

ROOSEVELT ELK / BULLS

Antlers are usually shed in March and new antlers begin growing in April.

April / Oregon

yellowish-white rump

"Spike" bull / August

Calves are born in May/June

Spotted coats are shed by summers end.

Birth weight - 30-40 pounds

Calf / July

ROOSEVELT ELK / CALVES

ROOSEVELT ELK / BULL (APRIL)

197

MOOSE

The moose (Alces alces) is the largest member of the deer family. In North America it is found from coast to coast throughout most of Alaska, Canada, and Newfoundland. South of the Canadian border they are found in the Rocky Mountain region south to Colorado. Maine, Minnesota, and Michigan (as well as other states, in smaller numbers) also have populations. Sometimes a moose will roam far from its "normal" range and become a local celebrity. Moose don't, however, normally migrate from their home-range, and if food is available will seldom leave their 5 square mile "home". During spring and summer the moose feeds on vegetation in ponds, grasses, and leaves of willows, aspen, and birch. In the winters they must sustain themselves on the twigs and bark of these trees. During winters of deep snow, moose often "herd up" to share their trail blazing, but starvation is always a threat to the younger and less able adults.

The moose is a large, brown creature that may stand 7 1/2' at the shoulder and be over 10' long. There are various subspecies of moose in North America and the Alaska race is the largest. A mature Alaskan male (bull) will weigh 1200 - 1600#'s and a female (cow) is usually about one-third smaller. This long-legged, droopy-nosed beast is well suited for the marshy, cold country it inhabits. A wild moose seldom survives over 15 years.

Only bulls grow antlers, and these huge racks may weigh 60#'s and be 5' - 6' wide. The "velvet" covering the antlers is shed in August/September and the annual "rut" usually peaks in October. During this time the largest bulls seldom feed and spend the months either fighting other bulls or mating with their harem of cows. This hectic period often depletes the bulls fat-reserves and they enter the harsh winters weak and undernourished; making themselves vulnerable to predators and starvation. Young (normally twins) are born the following May/June and these 25#, reddish-brown, un-spotted "calves" often weigh 250#'s by winter. Predators such as wolves, grizzlies, and Mountain lions take a toll, and usually only one calf survives the first few months. In Denali National Park (central Alaska) I know of areas where few calves survive due to the area grizzlies who have perfected the art of preying on vulnerable young moose.

BULL / IN "VELVET" (AUGUST)

Antlers are normally shed December-January

Bull Study / Alaska
November

MOOSE / BULLS

← Bell
(length & shape varies)
with age

MOOSE / COWS

TOP: MOOSE CALF (JUNE)   BOTTOM: MOOSE COW (JULY)   201

Bull track

←—— 6" ——→

Shed antler, January

MOOSE / BULLS

Broad "bells" on older bulls

MOOSE/BULL (AUGUST, ALASKA)

Young Bull
September

Average - 6½ - 7½'
at shoulder

Belly is 40" - 42" from
ground

Alaska

Dewclaw

MOOSE / BULL

205

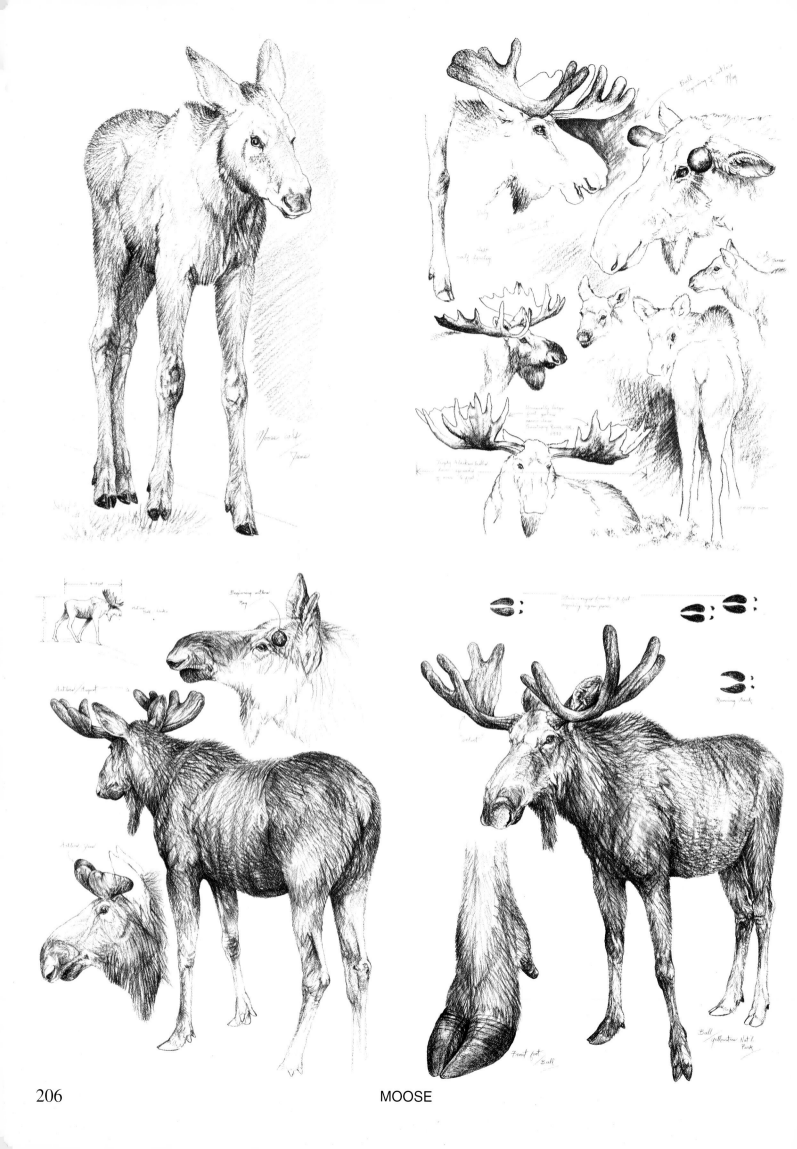

MOOSE

1 week old

Calf
3 weeks old
June

MOOSE / CALVES